50
CROCHET FLOWERS
Claire Crompton

Fresh looks for roses,
daisies, sunflowers
and more

Introduction

Crochet flowers are a perfect way to get to grips with this fun craft – once you've mastered the basics you can create beautiful yarn embellishments to adorn hats, scarfs, cushions or any soft-craft or papercraft project! This book offers a comprehensive collection of crochet stitches, ranging from the very simple to the more complex; the traditional to the innovative. Use it as an inspirational guide to making your own unique crocheted pieces, whether you are creating beautiful garments and accessories for yourself, or stylish adornments for your home.

Each section starts with a showcase of inspirational projects that offer you different ideas about how to use the designs; use these as a springboard for designing your own versions. Experiment with different yarn, textures and colours for truly unique flowers every time.

Basic Stitches

The designs in this book are created using only the basic crochet stitches. In this section we include useful reminders for how to make each stitch as well as ways they have been used in this book to generate different effects. We use US crochet terms here; for UK terms see the conversion table in the Following Crochet Patterns section.

Chain
(abbreviation = ch)

Every design in this book starts with a length of foundation chain. To make a motif, the length of chain is joined into a circle with a slip stitch. Chain stitches are also used to create lacy effects. The Snowflake motif is made entirely of chain lengths fixed with single crochet stitches.

Chain lengths can also make large spaces to be worked into.

Wrap the yarn around the hook from back to front. Pull the yarn through the loop on the hook. One chain stitch made. The pattern instructions will tell you how many to make; don't forget that the slip knot at the beginning doesn't count as a stitch.

Single crochet
(abbreviation = sc)

This is the shortest crochet stitch; by itself, it makes a dense fabric. It can be worked in rows to create a dense fabric stripe between lacier areas or combined with chain lengths. Single crochet is often combined with taller stitches to create wave or zigzag effects.

There will already be a loop on the hook, either from the foundation chain or from another stitch. Following the stitch instructions, insert the hook into the work at the correct position. Wrap the yarn around the hook from back to front and pull the yarn through the work on the hook.

Wrap the yarn around the hook from back to front again and pull through both loops on the hook. One single crochet made.

Double crochet
(abbreviation = dc)

This stitch is taller than the single crochet; it can make a dense fabric when
several stitches are worked together,
or a more open fabric when combined
with chain stitches. It also creates the
famous Granny crochet stitch, which
can be used as a fabric or a motif.

There will already be a loop on the
hook, either from the foundation
chain or from another stitch. Wrap
the yarn around the hook from back
to front then insert the hook into
the work at the correct position.
Wrap the yarn around the hook
from back to front and pull the
yarn through the work on the hook.
There are now three loops on
the hook.

Wrap the yarn around the hook
from back to front and pull
through the remaining two
loops on the hook. One double
crochet made.

Wrap the yarn around the hook
from back to front and pull through
the first two loops on the hook.

Half double crochet

(abbreviation = hdc)

The height of this stitch is halfway between the single and double crochet stitches. It isn't often used to make a fabric by itself but is effective when combined with other stitches. Sawtooth Fabric combines several heights of stitches together to create triangular blocks. Half double crochet is often used to shape flower petals such as the Large Simple Flower and the Four-Layer Flower, among many examples in this book.

Follow the instructions for the double crochet until there are three loops on the hook. Wrap the yarn around the hook from back to front and pull the yarn through all three loops. One half double crochet made.

Treble
(abbreviation = tr)

This stitch is taller than a double crochet and begins a series of very tall stitches that are used most effectively in lace fabrics or to create large open spaces. Combine trebles into clusters to create oversized fans of stitches, or use trebles as an easy way to make a lace fabric. The contrast in height can be seen in the petals of the Small Rose; the short ones worked in double crochet and the taller ones in treble stitches.

Wrap the yarn twice around the hook then insert the hook into the work at the correct position.

There are now three loops on the hook. Wrap the yarn around the hook and pull through the first two loops, leaving two loops on the hook.

Wrap the yarn around the hook and pull through the work – there are now four loops on the hook. Wrap the yarn around the hook and pull through the first two loops on the hook.

Finally, wrap the yarn around the hook from back to front and pull through the remaining two loops on the hook. One treble stitch made.

Taller treble variations

Double treble (abbreviation = dtr)
Triple treble (abbreviation = tr tr)

Taller stitches are made by wrapping the yarn around the hook more times before inserting it into the work. These tall stitches are used as fans or to make long pointed petals for the Pointed Daisy.

Double treble

Wrap the yarn three times around the hook before inserting it into the work. Follow the instructions for the treble stitch, starting by pulling the yarn through the work and then pulling it through two loops on the hook each time. You will do this one more time than the treble.

Triple treble

Wrap the yarn four times around the hook before inserting it into the work. Follow the instructions for the treble stitch, starting by pulling the yarn through the work and then pulling it through two loops on the hook each time. You will do this twice more than the treble.

Slip stitch
(abbreviation = sl st)

A working stitch with no height but many unseen uses. It is used to join the foundation chain into a circle to begin a motif, and close each round in a motif. It is used to move the hook to a new place without cutting yarn or adding height, to close picots;

or to fix long loops of chain stitches in place such as in the Loop Daisy.

There will already be a loop on the hook, either from the foundation chain or from another stitch. Insert the hook into the work at the correct position. Wrap the yarn around the hook from back to front and pull the yarn through both the work and the loop on the hook.
One slip stitch made.

More Complex Stitches

The basic stitches worked plainly on their own can create many varied crochet fabrics. But worked together into more complex stitches such as clusters, shells, fans and popcorns, they widen out the range of textures, lacy fabrics and colour effects that can be created and that are all featured in this book. Read the individual design instructions carefully, as a shell in one fabric may be different from a shell in another.

Shells and fans

These are two names for the same crochet element: a group of tall stitches spreading out from a single point. Both terms are used in the design instructions in this book. Fabrics can be made up entirely from shells, like the Treble Fans, or combined with other elements, such as with chain loops to make Shell and Net. A scalloped edging can be created along the edge of a garment by working the Simple Shell Edging or the Picot Shell edging, which has the extra frill of picots. The Damask Rose has petals made from shells.

Following the design instructions, make the required number of stitches into one point, usually a stitch or a chain.

Clusters

Clusters are the opposite of shells; a group of almost completed tall stitches spread across several points and then drawn together with a closing stitch. This creates an upside-down shell. Each stitch within the cluster is called a leg; the design instructions will tell you where to work each leg. A cluster can be made up of just a few stitches, like those used to make the petals on the Cluster Flower.

To make a cluster, work the individual stitches (or legs) up to the point where there are two loop on the hook – just before the stitch is completed. When all the individual legs have been made (three legs are shown in the artwork above), close the cluster by wrapping the yarn around the hook from back to front and pulling through all the loops on the hook.

If each leg is made up of a couple of stitches, the instructions may use a special abbreviation, such as '3 trnc'. This is explained in the written instructions.

Anywhere you see 'tog' in the written instructions or in the symbol key indicates a cluster; several stitches pulled together. A wide range of different 'tog' stitches are used in the stitch patterns, including sc2tog and sc3tog and tr2tog, tr3tog and tr4tog. The stitch type means you are working in sc (or tr), while the number is the number of stitches in the cluster (2, 3 or 4), and 'tog' shows it is a cluster. 'Tog' stitches are also used to make decreases to shape crochet fabric.

Puff stitches

This is a small bobble of stitches: a group of half-completed stitches worked in one point and then drawn together with a closing stitch. Puff stitches make very effective petals to a simple flower. Puff stitches are usually made from half double crochet stitches so they are short and dense, but always check the design instructions for variations.

There will already be a loop on the hook, either from the foundation chain or from another stitch. Wrap the yarn around the hook from back to front, then insert the hook into the work at the correct position. Wrap the yarn around the hook from back to front and pull the yarn through the work on the hook. There are now three loops on the hook. Make more stitches in the same way at the same point, according to the design instructions.

Wrap the yarn around the hook from back to front and pull through all the loops on the hook. One puff stitch made. Sometimes an extra chain stitch is worked to further close the puff stitch; check the design instructions.

Popcorns

These are worked in the same way as a shell, but when the shell is completed another closing stitch is worked to draw the shell up into a bobble. Although both elements create texture, a popcorn is different from a puff stitch in that it can be made from taller stitches and is larger.

Following the design instructions, work the required number of stitches in one point. Pull the last loop so it is bigger than usual and remove the hook. Carefully insert the hook through the top of the first stitch of the popcorn and then back into the enlarged end stitch. Pull the yarn to tighten this stitch again.

Wrap the yarn around the hook from back to front. Pull the yarn through both loops on the hook. One popcorn completed.

Picots

Picots are small decorative loops of chain stitches; they are a simple way to add a frill edge to any crocheted item. The simplest form is the Simple Picot Edging, which can be added to a plain crochet garment or to woven fabric as a decorative frill.

Following the design instructions, work to the point where the picot is to be made. Work the required number of chain. Insert the hook into the stitch at the beginning of the chain.

Wrap the yarn around the hook from back to front. To close with a slip stitch, pull the yarn through the work and the loop on the hook. To close with a single crochet, pull the yarn through the work on the hook, wrap the yarn around the hook from back to front and pull the yarn through both loops on the hook.

Following Crochet Patterns

The stitch patterns in this book have both written instructions and a chart. The instructions and diagrams can be used independently of each other, but referring to both can make it easier to work the design. Here we give some advice on following written crochet instructions; later we give advice on following charts.

Written Patterns

Each row or round (for the motifs) of the stitch patterns is written out; shorthand phrases are used to shorten the instructions and make them clearer. They refer to a set of instructions that must be repeated across a row or round.

Brackets

The repeated instructions may appear inside a set of round brackets: ( ). The number of times the instructions are repeated appears after the closing bracket.
For example: '(1 dc into next dc, 2 ch) 15 times.'

Asterisk

Sometimes for a long set of instructions an asterisk * is used. This marks the beginning of the repeat and is ended by the words 'rep from * to ...' This means you work across the instructions and then return to the asterisk and repeat them. You may be told how many times to do this or told to repeat to the end of the row or round, or to repeat to the last few stitches. The instructions may also tell you to repeat a certain number of times more. This means that you have already completed one repeat and so must repeat it that number of times again.
For example: '* 1 sc into each of next 5 dc, (1 sc, 3 ch, sl st into 3rd ch from hook, 1 sc) all into 2 ch sp; rep from * 7 times.'

OR: '* 1 sc into each of next 3 dc, 2 ch, miss 1 dc; rep from * 4 times more.'

OR: '* 2 sc into next 2 ch sp, 1 sc into next dc; rep from * to end.'

OR: '* 2 ch, miss 4 ch, 1 sc into next ch; rep from * to last 3 ch.'

Ending last repeat with...

Sometimes this is written as 'rep from * to end, ending with...' This means that the last repeat may be shorter or end differently than the previous repeats. Instead of writing out a lot of repeated instructions, this phrase is used to tell you how to end the last repeat.
For example: '* 1 sc into next ch, 5 ch, 1 sc into each of next 3 sc; rep from * to end, ending with 1 sc into each of last 2 sc.'

Into each of...

This phrase is used to replace writing out that the same stitch is worked into the next few stitches or chains below.
For example: '1 sc into next dc, 1 sc into next dc, 1 sc into next dc' is replaced by: '1 sc into each of next 3 dc.'

All into...

This is used to clarify that a lot of stitches are all going to be worked in the same place. Sometimes this is quite a lot of different stitches; they are written in brackets, so it is important to read to the end of the brackets to check where they will be worked.
For example: '(1 dc, 1 ch, 1 dc, 2 ch, 1 tr, 2 ch, 1 dc, 1 ch, 1 dc) all into next dc.'

Foundation chain

The stitch patterns are written in pattern repeats. The number of foundation chain you must make to begin the pattern is also written in pattern repeats; these are called multiples. Many of the stitch patterns also have an extra few chain that you must add after the multiples have been made.

For example: 'Make a foundation chain of a multiple of 16 ch plus an extra 9 ch.'

This means that for the pattern to work correctly, you must make a foundation chain of a multiple of 16; so 32, or 48, or 64, or 80, and so on. Then make an extra 9 chain to complete the foundation chain.

IMPORTANT: The slipknot does not count as one of the chain. So to begin, make a slipknot on your hook and then begin counting the foundation chain as you make them. The final chain will be the one on your hook.

Abbreviations

Abbreviations are used in crochet patterns to shorten commonly used terms so that the instructions are easier to read and a manageable length. The following is a list of all the abbreviations used in this book.

beg	beginning
ch	chain
ch sp(s)	chain space(s)
cm	centimetre(s)
dc	double crochet
dtr	double treble
foll	following
hdc	half double crochet
in	inch(es)
mm	millimetre
rep	repeat
rnd	round
RS	right side
sc	single crochet
sl st	slip stitch
sp(s)	space(s)
st(s)	stitch(es)
tch	turning chain
tog	together
tr	treble
trnc	treble not completed
tr tr	triple treble
WS	wrong side
yoh	yarn over hook

US and UK crochet terms

The stitch patterns in this book are written in US terms. These differ quite significantly from UK terms so care must be taken by UK and European crocheters that they work the correct stitches. Translating between the two can be confusing, as the same term can refer to different stitches under the different systems. One way to tell where you are is that the American system starts with a single crochet, which the UK system doesn't have; therefore any pattern with 'sc' in it can be identified as an American pattern. (To cause further confusion, some US patterns use the term 'triple' rather than 'treble', but we use 'treble' in this book.)

US	UK
single crochet (sc)	double crochet (dc)
half double crochet (hdc)	half treble (htr)
double crochet (dc)	treble (tr)s
treble (tr)	double treble (dtr)
double treble (dtr)	triple treble (tr tr)
triple treble (tr tr)	quadruple treble (qtr)

Crochet Charts

Each design in this book has its own chart. This is a visual representation of the stitch pattern; those worked in rows have a horizontal diagram of rows, while the motifs are a circle, square or hexagon. Each stitch is drawn and it is easy to see in which position it should be worked. The diagrams are read from the bottom to the top; the foundation chain is on the bottom edge, or, for motifs, the foundation ring will be in the centre. The charts are also printed in two colours. This makes the diagram easier to read, but doesn't mean that you have to change colour on every row or round.

Each type of stitch is represented by a different symbol. This symbol shows the height of the stitch, so the symbol for an sc is shorter

than the symbol for a tr. With each diagram, there is a key to explain what each symbol means. The same symbol is used to represent the most commonly used stitches in every diagram. Special or unusual stitches have their own symbols; similar symbols may mean slightly different things in different diagrams, so always check the key to make sure you work the stitch correctly. Stitches such as clusters or popcorns are drawn as they appear when you crochet them.

The rows or rounds are numbered and the pattern repeat is drawn along the foundation chain to show which part needs to be repeated. But always check with the written instructions, as the repeat can move to the left or right on different rows.

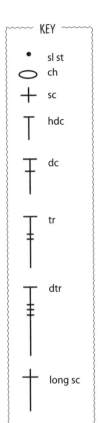

KEY

- • sl st
- ch
- sc
- hdc
- dc
- tr
- dtr
- long sc

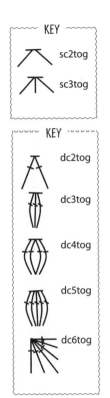

KEY

- sc2tog
- sc3tog

KEY

- dc2tog
- dc3tog
- dc4tog
- dc5tog
- dc6tog

KEY

- tr2tog
- ortr2tog
- tr3tog
- tr4tog

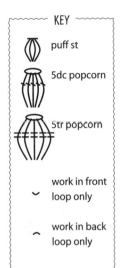

KEY

- puff st
- 5dc popcorn
- 5tr popcorn
- ⌣ work in front loop only
- ⌢ work in back loop only

flowers
flowers

Bunting

Floral bunting is easy to make and you can be really creative with yarns and colours. This project can be worked in one flower, or you could try mixing different flowers for a garland effect. This bunting is made in brightly coloured fine-weight mercerized cotton with a D3 (3.00mm) hook, using a Loop Daisy pattern. Join the flowers as you make them by working half a petal, inserting the hook through a petal of the previous flower, and then completing the petal.

Heart

A gift for Valentine's Day, this willow heart is decorated with two Small Roses and a Rose Bud made using two strands of dark red fine-weight mohair yarn and a D3 (3.00mm) hook. The three Leaves are made in a dark green lightweight silk and wool mix yarn with a G6 (4.00mm) hook. Sew the leaves onto the heart.

Corsage

A glitzy ready-made evening top is given even more sparkle with a corsage of three Open Roses. Refer to the pattern and use a lightweight metallic yarn in a toning shade with a D3 (3.00mm) hook. Sew the roses onto the neck edge. Alternatively, sew brooch pins onto the back of the flowers so they can be removed.

Necklace

Crochet flowers can be used to make simple but effective jewellery. This necklace is made from a Six-Petal Daisy pattern in three shades of lightweight purple wool using a D3 (3.00mm) hook. Cut a piece of waxed cord the length of necklace required. Make enough flowers to fit around the length; they can be grouped close together or spaced wider apart. Using a blunt needle, thread the flowers onto the cord, tying a knot at each side of the flower to prevent it slipping.

Bag decorations

Here a plain summer bag is brightened up with the addition of raffia flowers worked in shades of gold and green. Use a G6 (4.00mm) hook and the Ruffle Rose pattern. Work some of the flowers with two layers of petals and others with only one layer. Sew the flowers onto the bag.

Six-Petal Daisy

Make 2 ch.

Rnd 1 5 sc into 2nd ch from hook, sl st into 2nd of 2 ch to form a ring. 6 sc.

Rnd 2 (5 ch, 1 sc into 2nd ch from hook, 1 dc into each of next 2 ch,
1 hdc into last ch, sl st into next sc
of rnd 1) 6 times.

Fasten off.

~ KEY ~
· sl st
○ ch
+ sc
T hdc
‡ dc

Small Sunflower

Make 4 ch and join with sl st to form a ring.

Rnd 1 1 ch, 12 sc into ring, sl st to first sc.

Rnd 2 16 long sc into ring over scs of rnd 1, sl st into first sc.

Rnd 3 Working into back of loop only, 1 ch, 2 sc into same sc, 1 sc
into next sc, (2 sc into next sc, 1 sc into next sc) 7 times,
sl st into 1st sc. 24 sc.

Rnd 4 (3 ch, miss 1 sc, sl st into next sc) 12 times.

Fasten off.

~ KEY ~
^ in back
  of loop
· sl st
○ ch
+ sc
† long sc

Loop Daisy

Ruffle Rose

Make 2 ch.

Rnd 1 8 sc into 2nd ch from hook, sl st into 2nd of 2 ch to form a ring. 9 sc.

Rnd 2 2 ch (counts as 1 sc), 1 sc into same place, 2 sc into every sc to end, sl st into 2nd of 2 ch at beg of rnd. 18 sc.

Rnd 3 (10 ch, sl st into next sc) 18 times.

Fasten off.

Make 3 ch.

Rnd 1 11 dc into 3rd ch from hook, sl st into 3rd of 3 ch to form a ring. 12 dc.

Rnd 2 2 ch (counts as 1 sc), 1 sc into same sp, 2 sc into each of next 11 dc, sl st into 2nd of 2 ch. 24 sc.

Back layer of petals

Rnd 3 Working into back of loop only, 4 ch. 1 tr into same place, 2 tr into next sc, 1 tr into next sc, 4 ch, sl st into same sc, sl st into next sc, (4 ch, 1 tr into same sc, 2 tr into next sc, 1 tr into next sc, 4 ch, sl st into same sc, sl st into next sc) 7 times, working last sl st into first sc of rnd 2.

Front layer of petals

Rnd 4 Working into front of loop only, 3 ch, 1 dc into same place, 1 dc into next sc, 3 ch, sl st into same sc, sl st into next sc, (3 ch, 1 dc into same sc, 1 dc into next sc, 3 ch, sl st into same sc, sl st into next sc) 11 times, working last sl st into first sc of rnd 2.

Fasten off.

Open Rose

Small Rose

Make 4 ch and join with sl st to form a ring.

Rnd 1 2 ch (counts as 1 sc), 7 sc into ring, continue working in a spiral as follows: 2 sc into front of loop of 2nd of 2 at beg of rnd, 2 sc into front of loop of each of next 7 sc, 1 sc into front of loop of each of next 16 sc. 40 sc in total.

Turn work to reverse direction so WS is facing. Working into empty front of loop only and in a spiral from outer edge to centre, make a total of 20 petals [NB: chart shows first 8 petals only for guidance] as follows: 1 ch, (1 hdc, 3 dc, 1 hdc) into first sc, * 1 sc into next sc, (1 hdc, 3 dc, 1 hdc) into next sc; rep from * 18 times more, 1 sc into last sc.

Fasten off.

Make 36 ch.

Row 1 1 sc into 2nd ch from hook, 1 sc into each ch to end. 35 sc.

Row 2 3 ch, 3 dc into same sc, 3 ch, sl st into next sc, (3 ch, 3 dc into next sc, 3 ch, sl st into next sc) twice, (3 ch, 2 dc into each of next 2 sc, 3 ch, sl st into next sc) 3 times, (4 ch, 2 tr into each of next 3 sc, 4 ch, sl st into next sc) 5 times.

Fasten off.

Roll the strip up starting with the small petals at the centre. Secure with a few stitches sewn through all thicknesses.

KEY

	in front of loop
·	sl st
○	ch
+	sc
T	hdc
T̄	dc

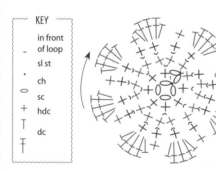

KEY

·	sl st
○	ch
+	sc
T	dc
T̄	tr

Rose Bud

Leaf

Make 16 ch.

Row 1 1 sc into 2nd ch from hook,
1 sc into each ch to end. 15 sc.

Row 2 3 ch, 3 dc into same sc, 3 ch, sl st into next sc, (3 ch, 3 dc into next sc, 3 ch, sl st into next sc) twice, (3 ch, 2 dc into each of next 2 sc, 3 ch, sl st into next sc) 3 times.

Fasten off.

Roll the strip up starting with the small petals at the centre. Secure with a few stitches sewn through all thicknesses.

Make 10 ch.

Rnd 1 1 sc into 2nd ch from hook,
1 hdc into next ch, 1 dc into next ch, 1 tr into each of next 3 ch, 1 dc into next ch, 1 hdc into next ch, 3 sc into last ch, continue back along other side of foundation ch as follows:
1 hdc into next ch, 1 dc into next ch, 1 tr into each of next 3 ch, 1 dc into next ch, 1 hdc into next ch, 1 sc into last ch.

Fasten off.

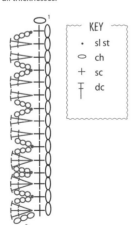

KEY

•	sl st
◦	ch
+	sc
T	dc

KEY

◦	ch
+	sc
T	hdc
T	dc
T	tr

Irish Crochet Rose

Make 4 ch and join with sl st to form a ring.

Rnd 1 3 ch (counts as 1 dc), 11 dc into ring, sl st to 3rd of 3 ch.

Rnd 2 1 ch, 1 sc into same place, 3 ch, * miss 1 dc, 1 sc into next dc, 3 ch; rep from * to end, sl st into first sc.

Rnd 3 * sl st into next 3 ch sp, (1 ch, 2 hdc, 1 dc, 2 hdc, 1 ch, sl st) all into same 3 ch sp; rep from * 5 times more.

Rnd 4 2 ch, sl st into first missed dc of rnd 2, 1 ch, 1 sc into same place, 4 ch, * 1 sc into next missed dc, 4 ch; rep from * to end, sl st into first sc.

Rnd 5 * sl st into next 4 ch sp, (1 ch, 1 hdc, 3 dc, 1 hdc, 1 ch, sl st) all into same 4 ch sp; rep from * 5 times more.

Fasten off.

KEY

•	sl st
◯	ch
+	sc
T	hdc
T̄	dc

Large Simple Flower

Make 4 ch and join with sl st to form a ring.

Rnd 1 3 ch (counts as 1 dc), 11 dc into ring, sl st to 3rd of 3 ch.

Rnd 2 * (1 ch, 1 hdc, 2 dc, 2 tr, 2 dc, 1 hdc, 1 ch) all into same place as sl st, miss next dc, sl st into next dc; rep from * 5 times more, working last sl st into first sl st.

Fasten off.

KEY

•	sl st
◯	ch
T	hdc
T̄	dc
T̄	tr

Star Flower

Pansy

Make 5 ch and join with sl st to form a ring.

Rnd 1 1 ch, 10 sc into ring, sl st to first sc.

Rnd 2 1 ch, 2 sc into each sc, sl st into first sc.

Rnd 3 (7 ch, 1 sc into 2nd ch from hook, 1 sc into next ch, 1 hdc into each of next 2 ch, 1 dc into each of next 2 ch, miss 1 sc of ring, sl st into next sc, turn work, 1 ch, 1 sc into each of next 2 dc, 1 sc into each of next 2 hdc, 1 sc into each of next 2 sc, turn, 1 ch, 1 sc into each of next 2 sc, 1 hdc into each of next 2 sc, 1 dc into each of next 2 sc, miss 1 sc of ring, sl st into next st) 5 times.

Fasten off.

Make 4 ch and join with sl st to form a ring.

Rnd 1 2 ch (counts as 1 hdc), 9 hdc into ring, sl st into first hdc.

Rnd 2 1 ch, 1 sc into same place, (3 ch, miss 1 hdc, 1 sc into next hdc) 4 times, 3 ch, miss 1 hdc, sl st to first sc.

Rnd 3 (sl st, 2 ch, 9 tr, 2 ch, sl st) all into each of first and second 3 ch sps, (sl st, 2 ch, 7 dc, 2 ch, sl st) all into each of next three 3 ch sps.

Fasten off.

KEY

·	sl st
○	ch
+	sc
T	hdc
ꟷ	dc
ꟷ	tr

KEY

·	sl st
○	ch
+	sc
T	hdc
ꟷ	dc

Dahlia

Make 2 ch.

Rnd 1 9 sc in 2nd ch from hook, join with sl st into first sc.

Rnd 2 4 ch, sl st into front of loop of first sc, (4 ch, sl st into front of loop of next sc) 8 times, sl st into first sl st.

Rnd 3 1 ch, 2 sc into back of loop of first sc, 2 sc into back of loop of each of next 8 sc, sl st into first sc.

Rnd 4 6 ch, sl st into front of loop of first sc, (6 ch, sl st into front of loop of next sc) 17 times more, sl st into first sl st.

Rnd 5 [NB: this rnd is not shown on chart but should be worked behind rnd 4] 8 ch, sl st into back of loop of first sc, (8 ch, sl st into back of loop of next sc) 17 times more.

Fasten off.

Four-Layer Flower

Make 2 ch.

Rnd 1 5 sc into 2nd ch from hook, sl st into front of loop of first sc.

Rnd 2 (1 sc, 1 ch, 1 sc, sl st) all into front of loop of first sc, (1 sc, 1 ch, 1 sc, sl st) all into front of loop of each of next 4 sc, working last sl st into back of loop of first sc.

Rnd 3 (2 ch, sl st in back of loop of next sc) 5 times.

Rnd 4 (sl st, 1 ch, 4 hdc, 1 ch, sl st) all into first 2 ch sp and into each of next four 2 ch sps.

Rnd 5 3 ch, sl st into back of petal between second and third hdc of first petal, (3 ch, sl st into back of next petal between second and third hdc) 5 times, ending with last sl st worked in first 3 ch sp.

Rnd 6 (1 ch, 1 hdc, 4 dc, 1 hdc, 1 ch, sl st) all into first 3 ch sp, (sl st, 1 ch, 1 hdc, 4 dc, 1 hdc, 1 ch, sl st) all into each of next four 3 ch sps.

Rnd 7 3 ch, sl st into back of petal between second and third dc of first petal, (4 ch, sl st into back of next petal between second and third dc) 5 times, ending with last sl st worked in first 4 ch sp.

Rnd 8 (sl st, 1 ch, 1 hdc, 6 dc, 1 hdc, 1 ch, sl st) all into first 4 ch sp, (sl st, 1 ch, 1 hdc, 6 dc, 1 hdc, 1 ch, sl st) all into each of next four 4 ch sps. Fasten off.

KEY

˅ in front of loop only

˄ in back of loop only

• sl st

○ ch

+ sc

KEY

˅ in front of loop only

˄ in back of loop only

• sl st

○ ch

+ sc

T hdc

ŦF dc

Trumpet Flower

Centre

Make 2 ch.

Rnd 1 6 sc into 2nd ch from hook, sl st to first sc.

Rnd 2 1 ch, 2 sc into each sc, sl st into first sc. 12 sc.

Rnd 3 1 ch, 1 sc into front of loop of each sc, sl st into first sc.

Rnd 4 1 ch, 1 sc into each sc, sl st into first sc.

Rnd 5 1 ch, 1 sc into first sc, 2 ch, (1 sc into next sc, 2 ch) 11 times, sl st to first sc.

Fasten off.

Petals

Rejoin yarn to back loop of any dc on row 3.

Rnd 6 1 ch, 1 sc into same place, (2 ch, 1 sc into back of loop of each of next 2 sc) 5 times, 2 ch, 1 sc into back of loop of last sc, sl st to first sc.

Rnd 7 Sl st into first 2 ch sp, * (1 ch, 1 hdc, 1 dc, 1 tr, 1 dc, 1 hdc, 1 ch) all into 2 ch sp, sl st between next 2 sc; rep from * 5 times more.

Rnd 8 * Sl st into 1 ch sp of petal, (2 ch, sl st into next st) 5 times, 2 ch, sl st into last 1 ch sp of petal; rep from * 5 times more.

Fasten off.

Frilly Rosette

Make 4 ch and join with sl st to form a ring.

Rnd 1 1 ch, 6 sc into ring, sl st into back of loop of 1st sc.

Rnd 2 1 ch, 2 sc into back of loop of each sc, sl st into back of loop of 1st sc. 12 sc.

Rnd 3 1 ch, 2 sc into back of loop of each sc, sl st into back of loop of 1st sc. 24 sc.

Rnd 4 1 ch, 1 sc into back of loop of each sc, sl st into back of loop of 1st sc.

Rnd 5 (14 ch, 1 sc into back of loop of next sc) 24 times, (10 ch, 1 sc into front of loop of next sc) 24 times. Two layers of petals on outer rnd [NB: only the first layer of petals is shown on the chart].

Rnd 6 1 ch, 1 sc into front of loop of next sc on rnd 3, (6 ch, 1 sc into front of loop of next sc) 24 times.
Fasten off.

KEY	
~	in front of loop
⌒	in back of loop
•	sl st
◯	ch
+	sc

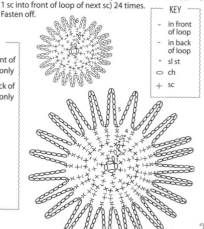

KEY	
~	in front of loop only
⌒	in back of loop only
•	sl st
◯	ch
+	sc
T	hdc
⊤	dc
‡	tr

Quick Flower

Button Carnation

Make 4 ch and join with sl st to form a ring.

Rnd 1 3 ch (counts as 1 dc), 11 dc into ring, sl st to 3rd of 3 ch. 12 dc.

Rnd 2 1 ch, 1 sc into same place, (4 ch, 1 dc into 4th ch from hook, miss 1 dc, 1 sc into next dc) 6 times, omitting last sc, instead ending with sl st into first sc.

Fasten off.

Make 2 ch.

Rnd 1 6 sc into 2nd ch from hook, sl st into first sc.

Rnd 2 1 ch, 2 sc into each of 6 sc, sl st into first sc. 12 sc.

Rnd 3 1 ch, 1 sc into each of next 12 sc, sl st into first sc.

Rnd 4 1 ch, (1 sc into each of next 2 sc, sc2tog) 3 times, sl st into first sc. 9 sc.

Rnd 5 (2 ch, 1 dc, 1 ch, 1 tr, 1 ch, 1 dc, 2 ch, sl st into same sc, sl st into next sc) 9 times.

Fasten off.

KEY
· sl st
○ ch
+ sc
┬ dc

KEY
· sl st
○ ch
+ sc
⅄ sc2tog
┬ dc
┬ tr

Pointed Daisy

Make 4 ch and join with sl st to form a ring.

Rnd 1 3 ch (counts as 1 dc), 11 dc into ring, sl st into first dc. 12 dc.

Rnd 2 1 ch, 1 sc into same place, (2 ch, miss 1 dc, 1 sc into next dc) 5 times, 2 ch, sl st into first dc.

Rnd 3 Sl st in 1st 2 ch sp, *(1 ch, 1 sc, 2 ch, 1 tr, 3 dtr, 1 tr, 2 ch, 1 sc, 1 ch) all into same 2 ch sp, sl st into next 2 ch sp; rep from * 5 times more, sl st to first sc.

Rnd 4 * Sl st into first 2 ch sp, 2 sc into same 2 ch sp, 1 sc into each of next 2 sts, (1 sc, 3 ch, sl st into 3rd ch from hook, 1 sc) all into next st, 1 sc into each of next 2 sts, 2 sc into 2 ch sp, sl st into ch between petals; rep from * 5 times more.

Fasten off.

Traditional Crochet Flower

Make 4 ch and join with sl st to form a ring.

Rnd 1 1 ch, 8 sc into ring, sl st into front of loop of first sc.

Rnd 2 (3 ch, sl st into front of loop of next sc) 8 times.

Rnd 3 (1 ch, 2 sc, 1 ch, sl st) all into first 3 ch sp, (sl st, 1 ch, 2 sc, 1 ch, sl st) all into each of next seven 3 ch sps.

Rnd 4 2 ch, 2 dc into back of loop of first sc on rnd 3, 2 dc into back of loop of each sc, sl st to first dc.

Rnd 5 (3 ch, sl st into next dc) 16 times.

Rnd 6 (1 ch, 2 sc, 1 ch, sl st) all into first 3 ch sp, (sl st, 1 ch, 2 sc, 1 ch, sl st) all into each of next fifteen 3 ch sps. Fasten off.

KEY

- • sl st
- ○ ch
- + sc
- ⊤ dc
- | tr
- ‡ dtr

KEY

- ⌃ in back of loop
- ⌄ in front of loop
- • sl st
- ○ ch
- + sc
- ⊤ dc

Gerbera

Make 6 ch and join with sl st to form a ring.

Rnd 1 1 ch, 12 sc into ring, sl st to first sc.

Rnd 2 1 ch, 1 sc into first sc, (16 ch, 1 sc into next sc) 11 times, 16 sc, sl st to first sc.

Rnd 3 Into each 16 ch loop work as follows: 1 sl st into each of first 3 ch, 1 sc into each of next 4 ch, 2 sc into each of next 2 ch, 1 sc into each of next 4 ch, 1 sl st into each of next 3 ch.

Fasten off.

Button Daisy

Make 2 ch.

Rnd 1 6 sc into 2nd ch from hook, sl st into first sc.

Rnd 2 1 ch, 2 sc into each of next 6 sc, sl st into first sc. 12 sc.

Rnd 3 1 ch, 1 sc into each of next 12 sc, sl st into first sc.

Rnd 4 1 ch, (1 sc into each of next 2 sc, sc2tog) 3 times, sl st to first sc. 9 sc.

Rnd 5 (6 ch, sl st into 2nd ch from hook, 1 sc into each of next 2 ch, 1 hdc into next ch, 1 dc into next ch, sl st into next sc or sc2tog) 9 times.

Fasten off.

KEY

- • sl st
- ◯ ch
- ✕ sc

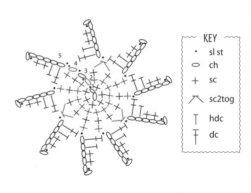

KEY

- • sl st
- ◯ ch
- ✕ sc
- ⋀ sc2tog
- ⊤ hdc
- ⊤ dc

Open Flower

Make 4 ch and join with sl st to form a ring.

Rnd 1 1 ch, 7 sc into ring, sl st into first sc.

Rnd 2 1 ch, 2 sc into each of next 7 sc, sl st to first sc. 14 sc.

Rnd 3 1 ch, (1 sc into next sc, 2 ch, 1 dc into next sc, 2 ch) 7 times, sl st to first sc.

Fasten off.

KEY
- • sl st
- ○ ch
- + sc
- ⊤ dc

Small Orchid

Make 2 ch.

Rnd 1 6 sc into 2nd ch from hook, sl st into first sc. 6 sc.

Rnd 2 (4 ch, 1 sc into 2nd ch from hook, 1 hdc into next ch, 1 sc into next ch, sl st into front of loop of next sc) 6 times, ending by working sl st into back of loop of first sc.

Rnd 3 1 ch, 2 sc into back of loop of each of next 6 sc, sl st into first sc. 12 sc.

Rnd 4 (5 ch, 1 sc into 2nd ch from hook, 1 hdc into next ch, 1 dc into next ch, 1 tr into next ch, miss 1 sc of rnd 3, sl st into back of loop of next sc) 6 times.

Fasten off.

KEY
- ⌣ in front of loop
- ⌢ in back of loop
- • sl st
- ○ ch
- + sc
- ⊤ hdc
- ⊤ dc
- ⊤ tr

Cluster Flower

Picot Daisy

Make 6 ch and join with sl st to form a ring.

Rnd 1 (3 ch, tr3tog, 3 ch, sl st into ring) 5 times.

Fasten off.

Make 5 ch and join with sl st to form a ring.

Rnd 1 1 ch, (1 sc into ring, 5 ch) 5 times, sl st to first sc.

Rnd 2 * 3 ch, 4 tr into 5 ch sp, 3 ch, sl st into sc; rep from * 4 times more.

Rnd 3 * 2 ch, sl st into 3 ch sp, (3 ch, sl st into 3rd ch from hook, sl st into next tr) 4 times, 3 ch, sl st into 3rd ch from hook, sl st into 3 ch sp, 2 ch, sl st into sl st between petals; rep from * 4 times more.

Fasten off.

KEY
- • sl st
- ◦ ch
- tr3tog

KEY
- • sl st
- ◦ ch
- + sc
- tr

Large Gerbera

Make 6 ch and join with sl st to form a ring.

Rnd 1 1 ch, 14 sc into ring, sl st to first sc.

Rnd 2 1 ch, in front of loop of each sc work (1 sc, 6 ch, 1 sc), sl st to first sc.

Rnd 3 1 ch, in back of loop of each sc work (1 sc, 8 ch, 1 sc), sl st to first sc.

Fasten off.

Damask Rose

Make 39 ch.

Row 1 1 dc into 6th ch from hook, * 1 ch, miss 2 ch, (1 dc, 2 ch, 1 dc) all into next ch; rep from * to end.

Row 2 3 ch (counts as 1 dc), (1 dc, 2 ch, 2 dc) all into 1st 2 ch sp, * 2 ch, (2 dc, 2 ch, 2 dc) all into next 2 ch sp; rep from * to end.

Row 3 3 ch (counts as 1 dc), 5 dc into first 2 ch sp, (1 sc into next 2 ch sp, 6 dc into next 2 ch sp) twice, (1 sc into next 2 ch sp, 8 dc into next 2 ch sp) 4 times, (1 sc into next 2 ch sp, 10 dc into next 2 ch sp) 5 times.

Fasten off, leaving a long tail for sewing up.

Thread the long tail onto a needle. Roll the petals up from the centre, beginning with the small petals. Sew through all layers at the base to secure.

Long Star Flower

Blossom

Make 3 ch.

Rnd 1 19 dc into 3rd ch from hook, sl st to top of 3 ch to form a ring.

Rnd 2 * 10 ch, 1 sc into 2nd ch from hook, 1 sc into each of next 8 ch, 1 sc into each of next 2 dc; rep from * to end, sl st to first sc.

Fasten off.

Make 5 ch and join with sl st to form a ring.

Rnd 1 2 ch, dc2tog into same place (counts as 1 dc3tog), 5 dc3tog into ring, sl st to top of first dc3tog.

Rnd 2 (1 ch, 3 dc, 1 ch, sl st all into top of dc3tog, sl st into top of next dc3tog) 6 times.

Fasten off.

KEY	
•	sl st
⌒	ch
+	sc
†	dc

KEY	
•	sl st
⌒	ch
†	dc
⫼	dc3tog

Simple Picot Flower

Make 4 ch and join with sl st to form a ring.

Rnd 1 1 ch, 8 sc into ring, sl st to first sc.

Rnd 2 7 ch, sl st into 3rd ch from hook, 1 ch, 1 dc into sc at base of
7 ch, 1 ch, (1 dc, 4 ch, sl st into 3rd ch from hook, 1 ch, 1 dc, 1 ch) all into each of next 7 sc, sl st to 3rd of 7 ch.

Fasten off.

Four-Petal Flower

Make 2 ch.

Rnd 1 7 sc into 2nd ch from hook, sl st into 2nd of 2 ch to form a ring. 8 sc.

Rnd 2 * 2 ch, (1 dc, 3 ch, sl st into 3rd ch from hook, 1 dc) all into next sc, 2 ch, sl st into next sc; rep from * 3 times more.

Fasten off.

```
KEY
 •  sl st
 ◠  ch
 +  sc
 ╤  dc
```

```
KEY
 •  sl st
 ◠  ch
 +  sc
 ╤  dc
```

Five-Petal Flower

Make 2 ch.

Rnd 1 9 sc into 2nd ch from hook, sl st into 2nd of 2 ch to form a ring. 10 sc.

Rnd 2 1 ch, 1 sc into same place, 2 sc into each of next 9 sc, 1 sc into same place as first sc, sl st to first sc. 20 sc.

Rnd 3 (3 ch, tr2tog worked over next 2 sc, 3 ch, sl st into each of next 2 sc) 5 times, ending with 1 sl st into first sc.

Fasten off.

KEY
- sl st
- ○ ch
- + sc
- 𝄫 tr2tog

Eight-Petal Flower

Make 4 ch and join with sl st to form a ring.

Rnd 1 1 ch, 1 sc into ring, (3 ch, 1 sc) 7 times into ring, 1 ch, 1 dc into first 3 ch sp.

Rnd 2 1 ch, 1 sc into top of dc, (4 ch, sl st into 3rd ch from hook, 1 ch, 1 sc into next 3 ch sp) 8 times, ending with sl st into first sc.

Fasten off.

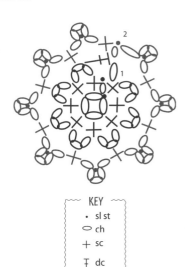

KEY
- sl st
- ○ ch
- + sc
- 𝕋 dc

Large Cluster Flower

Make 4 ch and join with sl st to form a ring.

Rnd 1 3 ch, 1 tr into ring (counts as 1 tr2tog), (3 ch, 1 tr2tog into ring) 5 times, 3 ch, sl st into top of first tr.

Rnd 2 1 ch, (1 sc, 1 hdc, 3 dc, 1 hdc, 1 sc) all into first 3 ch sp and into each of next five 3 ch sps.

Fasten off.

Button Gerbera

Make 4 ch and join with sl st to form a ring.

Rnd 1 2 ch, dc2tog into ring (counts as 1 dc3tog), five dc3tog into ring, sl st to first dc3tog.

Rnd 2 (4 ch, 1 sc into 2nd ch from hook, 1 hdc into next ch, 1 dc into next ch, sl st to top of next dc3tog) 6 times.

Fasten off.

KEY	
·	sl st
○	ch
+	sc
T	hdc
Ŧ	dc
⋔	tr2tog

KEY	
·	sl st
○	ch
+	sc
T	hdc
Ŧ	dc
⋔	dc3tog

Hellebore

Make 5 ch and join with sl st to form a ring.

Rnd 1 3 ch (counts as 1 dc), 14 dc into ring, sl st to first dc.

Rnd 2 * 2 ch, 1 dc into same place, 3 dc into next dc, (1 dc, 2 ch, sl st) all into next dc, sl st into next dc; rep from * 4 times more.

Fasten off.

KEY
- · sl st
- ⊖ ch
- ∓ dc

Traditional Crochet Rose

Make 4 ch and join with sl st to form a ring.

Rnd 1 1 ch, 6 sc into ring, sl st to first sc.

Rnd 2 1 ch, 1 sc into same sc, (3 ch, 1 sc into next sc) 5 times, 3 ch, sl st into first sc.

Rnd 3 Sl st into first 3 ch sp, (1 sc, 3 hdc, 1 sc, sl st) all into same 3 ch sp, (sl st, 1 sc, 3 hdc, 1 sc, sl st) all into each of next five 3 ch sps.

Fasten off.

KEY
- · sl st
- ⊖ ch
- + sc
- T hdc

Sunflower

Make 4 ch and join with sl st to form a ring.

Rnd 1 3 ch (counts as 1 dc), 9 dc into ring, sl st to 3rd of 3 ch. 10 dc.

Rnd 2 1 ch, (1 sc, 3 ch, sl st into 3rd ch from hook, 1 sc) all into first dc, * 3 ch, sl st into 3rd ch from hook, (1 sc, 3 ch, sl st into 3rd ch from hook, 1 sc) all into next sc; rep from * 9 times more, sl st to first sc.

Fasten off.

Irish Crochet Leaf

Make 8 ch.

Row 1 1 sc into 2nd ch from hook, 1 sc into each of next 5 ch, 5 sc into last ch, working along other side of foundation ch, 1 sc into each of next 6 ch, 3 sc into next ch, 1 sc into each of next 5 sc.

Row 2 1 ch, 1 sc into each of next 6 sc, 3 sc into next sc, 1 sc into each of next 6 sc.

Row 3 1 ch, 1 sc into each of next 7 sc, 3 sc into next sc, 1 sc into each of next 5 sc.

Row 4 1 ch, 1 sc into each of next 6 sc, 3 sc into next sc, 1 sc into each of next 6 sc.

Fasten off.

Four-Leaf Sprig

Fern Leaf

Make 5 ch.

Row 1 1 ch, 1 sc into 2nd ch from hook, 1 sc into each of next 3 ch, (6 ch, 1 sc into 2nd ch from hook, 1 hdc into next ch, 1 dc into next ch, 1 hdc into next ch, 1 sc into next ch, sl st into next ch) 3 times.

Fasten off.

Make 8 ch.

1st leaf 1 sc into 2nd ch from hook, 1 hdc into next ch, 1 dc into next ch, 2 ch, sl st into next ch.

2nd leaf 6 ch, 1 sc into 2nd ch from hook, 1 hdc into next ch, 1 dc into next ch, 2 ch, sl st into next ch.

3rd leaf 4 ch, 1 sc into 2nd ch from hook, 1 hdc into next ch, 1 dc into next ch, 2 ch, sl st into same ch at end of previous leaf.

4th leaf 4 ch, 1 sc into 2nd ch from hook, 1 hdc into next ch, 1 dc into next ch, 2 ch, sl st into same ch at end of previous leaf.

5th leaf Sl st into each of next 2 ch, sl st into same ch as first leaf, 4 ch, 1 sc into 2nd ch from hook, 1 hdc into next ch, 1 dc into next ch, 2 ch, sl st into same ch as first leaf, sl st into each of next 4 ch.

Fasten off.

KEY

- • sl st
- ○ ch
- + sc
- T hdc
- T̲ dc

KEY

- • sl st
- ○ ch
- + sc
- T hdc
- T̲ dc

3rd leaf

2nd leaf

4th leaf

5th leaf

1st leaf

Picot Leaf

Puff Stitch Flower

Picot 3 ch, sl st into 3rd ch from hook

Make 15 ch.

Row 1 1 sc into 2nd ch from hook, * make a picot, 1 sc into next ch, 1 hdc into next ch, make a picot, 1 hdc into next ch, 1 dc into next ch, (make a picot, 1 dc into each of next 2 ch) twice, make a picot, 1 dc into next ch, 1 hdc into next ch, make a picot, 1 hdc into next ch, 1 sc into next ch, make a picot, * (2 sc, make a picot, 2 sc) into last ch.

Row 2 Working along the other side of foundation ch, rep from * to *, 1 sc into last ch.

Fasten off.

Make 4 ch and join with sl st to form a ring.

Rnd 1 * 2 ch, work a puff st as follows: (yoh, insert hook into ring, yoh, pull a loop through) 4 times, yoh, pull through all 9 loops on hook, 2 ch, sl st into ring; rep from * 4 times more.

Fasten off.

KEY

- sl st
- ∘ ch
- ⑩ puff st

KEY

- · sl st
- ∘ ch
- + sc
- T hdc
- Ŧ dc

Simple Loop Flower

Make 4 ch and join with sl st to form a ring.

Rnd 1 1 ch, 8 sc into ring, sl st into first sc. 8 sc.

Rnd 2 (3 ch, sl st into next sc) 8 times.

Fasten off.

KEY

. sl st

○ ch

+ sc

Six-Petal Flower

Make 6 ch and join with sl st to form a ring.

Rnd 1 1 ch, (1 sc, 4 ch, 1 sc into ring) 6 times, sl st into first sc.

Rnd 2 1 ch, (6 sc into 4 ch sp, sl st between 2 sc of previous rnd) 6 times.

Fasten off.

KEY

. sl st

○ ch

+ sc

Carnation

Make 6 ch and join with sl st to form a ring.

Rnd 1 1 ch, 15 sc into ring, sl st into first sc. 15 sc.

Rnd 2 3 ch (counts as 1 dc), 2 dc into same sc, 3 dc into each of next 14 sc, sl st into 3rd of 3 ch at beg of rnd. 45 tr.

Rnd 3 3 ch (counts as 1 dc), 2 dc into same dc, 3 dc into each of next 44 dc, sl st into 3rd of 3 ch at beg of rnd. 135 dc.

Rnd 4 * 4 ch, sl st into next dc; rep from * to end.

Fasten off.

Chrysanthemum

Make 6 ch and join with sl st to form a ring.

Rnd 1 1 ch, 15 sc into ring, sl st into first dc. 15 sc.

Front layer of petals

Rnd 2 Working into front of loop only, (8 ch, sl st into 2nd ch from hook, sl st into each of next 6 ch, sl st into next sc) 14 times, 8 ch, sl st into 2nd ch from hook, sl st into each of next 6 ch, sl st into back of next sc.

Back layer of petals

Rnd 3 Working into back of loop only, 1 ch, 2 sc into each of next 15 sc, sl st to first sc. 30 sc.

Rnd 4 (8 ch, sl st into 2nd ch from hook, sl st into each of next 6 ch, sl st into next sc) 30 times.

Fasten off.

KEY	
·	sl st
○	ch
+	sc
⊤	dc

KEY	
·	sl st
○	ch
+	sc
⌄	in front of loop only
⌃	in back of loop only

Acknowledgments

I would like to thank the following people who have worked so hard to produce this book. Nicola Hodgson for her hard work, attention to detail and wonderful editing skills. Jack Kirby and Lorna Yabsley for their gorgeous photography, and the models for wearing the garments and accessories so beautifully. And finally everyone at David & Charles, including Jennifer Fox-Proverbs, James Brooks, Charly Bailey and Sarah Clark.

About the Author

Claire Crompton has worked in the knitting industry for over 20 years. After a Knitwear Design degree, she became a crochet and knitting pattern designer for a major yarn manufacturer. She has now established her own range of patterns and teaches workshops around the UK. Claire is the author of the best-selling The Knitter's Bible which began a series including Knitted Bags, Knitted Accessories, Knitted Throws and Cushions, and Stitch Library. See Claire's website for more information:

www.clairecrompton.co.uk